Praise for Irene Marques

T0278573

"*The Perfect Unravelling of the Spirit* [Mawenzi House, 2012] ties the secular rituals of everyday to sacred rites of passage, binding language to love and longing, and to the livelihoods that are Irene Marques's birthright. These poems bring new and old worlds into dialogue, and poetry into the presence of timeless, generous spirits."

—J Edward Chamberlin,
Professor Emeritus of English and Comparative Literature,
University of Toronto

"What impresses most in Irene Marques's first book of poetry, *Wearing Glasses of Water* [Mawenzi House, 2007], are the expansive situations she creates. Rarely does small abide over large, or unadorned show instead of ornate, for this Portuguese-born Canadian writer revels in abundance and lush colorings. Call this fat poetry, not thin. At its best it reminds me of the magic realism of Gabriel Garcia Marquez: everything writ large and interconnected. Marques continually welcomes us into her world with poetic leis and figurative dances. We come to recognize her through over-exposure, exaggeration, generous sloppiness, and glee. The poems knit together with repeated images and words so that the whole assumes a universal feel . . . Marques has a clear ability to turn a poem and make it her own."

—*Arc Poetry Magazine*

"The essence of Marques's poetry is a peep into the complex dimensions and psychological states of being, of creativeness and inventiveness with the Word, of themes and motifs of libidinal drives or instincts, of internal emotional conflicts where individual impulses and needs must be placed in ethical resolution with social or moral obligations. [With] Irene Marques and *Wearing Glasses of Water* [Mawenzi House, 2007], the world is consequently geared for renewal, the universe set to expand in its revolving and perpetuating order—an order that needs must leave behind for all humanity a glow of transformation. Thenceforth we can strive in wearing our teardrops, ("glasses of water") knowing that life deals these experiences to us in an effort to imbue meaning and purpose to terrestrial existence, which also means—as some of our own poets would hint—our filling the higher ethics to the craft and aesthetes of our various creative calling."

—*African Journal of New Poetry*

"*Uma Casa no Mundo* is a novel of solid structure that addresses themes of high significance: learning, memory and a diffused relation with History. In Irene Marques's novel, the reader is exposed to an important part of Portugal's History spanning approximately one century of colonial history in Africa and ending with the April Revolution, which led to the abolishment of the Portuguese dictatorship, and ultimately also the independence of the African colonies. Moreover, the novel also exposes the reader to relevant psychological portraits of the Portuguese people as they deal with their own individual reality and external realities that affect their lives. Yet, the whole narrative is presented to us in an involving manner through an eminently human lens where the story, the traits and universe of each character gradually reveal the sociopolitical situation, and ensuing dramas and traumas. We are in the presence of a novel that allows for a historical and social reading of a country, while at the same time providing us with a direct depiction of humans as they engage and deal with war, face physical and psychological misery, and suffer the brutality that arises as men dominate other men. And through all this, we also see at work the power of fraternal and romantic love, and the human desire for fulfillment—universal and intemporal themes. On the other hand, Irene Marques's narrative style in this novel skillfully ties social realism with the fantastic, giving the text a universal tone and quality, showing any reader that which is essentially human, no matter the latitude we inhabit."

—Jury, Prémio Imprensa Nacional Ferreira de Castro

The Bare Bones of Our Alphabet

poetry

Irene Marques

MAWENZI
HOUSE

Copyright ©2024 Irene Marques

Except for purposes of review, no part of this book may be reproduced in any form without prior permission of the publisher.

We acknowledge the support of the Canada Council for the Arts for our publishing program. We also acknowledge support from the Government of Ontario through the Ontario Arts Council, and the support of the Government of Canada through the Canada Book Fund.

Cover design by Sabrina Pignataro
Cover image by everything bagel / Shutterstock
Author photo by Abramovici Studios

The following poems have previously been published as follows:

"My Toenails," "There are No Words," and "I Do Not Speak" in *Gávea-Brown: A Bilingual Journal of Portuguese-North American Letters and Studies* 47, 2020.

"Small Words," "The Kitchen," "Notions of God," and "The Gemini in Me" in *Portuguese Literary and Cultural Studies: Luso-American Literatures and Cultures Today* 32, 2019.

"Verbs," "This Love, This Light," "A Dreamed Grammar," and "You—" in *Maple Tree Literary Supplement* 23, 2018.

"The Theory of Lungs" by AngelHousePress for National Poetry Month, 2023.

Library and Archives Canada Cataloguing in Publication

Title: The bare bones of our alphabet : poetry / Irene Marques.
Names: Marques, Irene, 1969- author.
Identifiers: Canadiana (print) 20240363973 | Canadiana (ebook) 20240363981 | ISBN 9781774151655 (softcover) | ISBN 9781774151662 (EPUB) | ISBN 9781774151679 (PDF)
Subjects: LCGFT: Poetry.
Classification: LCC PS8626.A68 B37 2024 | DDC C811/.6—dc23

Printed and bound in Canada by Coach House Printing

Mawenzi House Publishers Ltd.
39 Woburn Avenue (B)
Toronto, Ontario M5M 1K5
Canada

www.mawenzihouse.com

To those who use the word with care
and are open to its benign powers.

To my mother and father who taught me poetry:
the poetry of a life that was difficult but also beautiful.

"But given that we have to write, we shall at the very least not annihilate the blank spaces with words."

CLARICE LISPECTOR

"Why only one song, one speech, one text at a time?"

LUCE IRIGARAY

Contents

Note to the Reader

Dear reader,

Like others have said before me, poetry should transmit an intimation of significance. I too, believe that and I hope that you find in my words, intimations and insights that will speak to you in various ways, will guide you in some of your daily struggles. The traditional role of poetry is also to allow the release of intense emotions, an aspect that I also honour when I write poetry. Intense emotions are necessary: whether they are joyful or painful, we have to honour them, without feeling that we are being the spoiler of the party. As Clarice Lispector puts it, "But it is not always necessary to be strong. We must respect our weakness. Then our tears become gentle with that legitimate sadness to which we are entitled" (in *Discovering the World*). And so, I invite you to feel with me, to allow yourself to experience the multiplicity of emotions that you, as a human being, are called to experience in a world that demands, confuses, compartmentalizes and lacerates our soul. In that sense, my writing is also concerned with accessing deep modes of communication and paying attention to emotion, spiritual and non-rational ways of apprehending truth in order to bypass superficial levels of interaction and understanding. These intelligences are presented as sources of great potential to address social problems and allow personal growth and consciousness expansion.

The poems address universal themes and contemporary issues such as women's oppression (tied to normalized patriarchal rhetoric), poverty, exploitation and the importance of an ethics of truth in communication to bring about global change and equality in a world that relies too much on a deceptive language centered around capitalism and individualism. This book came out of my deep desire for an honest and ethical language. Whether one is dealing with family members, a lover, a co-worker, a cat, or a tree, whether in public and private, language matters, and we are responsible for its use. Language is often used to manipulate, hide, attain personal benefit, appease the current political moment, where freedom, ethics and concern for others or otherness (the planet/the non-human) are constantly evoked, and yet it often feels like a performance that has little substance. Honest, deep, and multifaceted communication is presented as necessary to build a healthier world. What I seek, ask for, and work obsessively to tap into is a native tongue, a vernacular that bypasses the traps of a supposed rationality and objectivity forged in a body politic consumed by self-interests that reduce our ontological experience.

IRENE MARQUES

The Gemini in Me

I am a Gemini. Full of selves: well, two selves at least—my father and my mother. From my father I possess a poetic undertone: I inherited his love for proverbs, those wise words told to him by his father who heard it from his grandmother—a line that never ends. Words and words travelling down, from the very beginning, when humans started to think about how to express their love for one another through clean syllables—likely because they felt lonely and it was the way to the self. He, my father, also gave me the capacity to feel, very deeply, the earth in my bones: the astonishing and vibrant power of the spring, the warm darkness of the winter and the milder feelings of the other two seasons in every fiber of my body so that I fully feel I am a being of the land. My mother is another story: mama of ten children, she had to think complicated thoughts to explain the complication that her life came to be. The dialectics of her oppression got enmeshed in the Hegelian twisted philosophical ideology of the one who slaves and the one who masters and all the ensuing confrontations that arise from such disagreeable dichotomies. She passed this hindrance to me making me more intellectual than I in fact wish to be, for in being more intellectual, I lose my natural ways of life: to love just because one loves, to be just because one is fundamentally a being who fundamentally is. I wish I could only follow my father's inheritance and feel like a true daughter of this earth, speak that language that emerged at the beginning as a way to tell the other the love we feel. This does not mean that I can renounce my mother. I cannot, for I am truly her daughter.

Verbs

I had a verb in my hand. It landed there, spat through my insatiable tongue after nights and nights of crouching on the floor, my knees bleeding, a suffering saint, praying, waiting for miracles to appear: like tall, incendiary monuments, columns visible to the eye, touchable by hand. My Apollo certain and languid in erected muscles licking my bones into a nothingness that I adore. I, no longer waiting for the concrete, because you had given it to me through that strong body of verbs that broke my isolation into one thousand pieces. All because of those verbs, of your own making, magnificent words of doing that you let out from the depths of your dreaming entrails, that core covered by skin where the most ancient beings, the bacteria of primal life, dance incessantly and produce birds and flowers and stars—and that body of yours, tall, erect and strong that you extend to me in moments of utter certainty and love for all the animals of the world. The bones, the bread, all the living beings. My breathing darling alphabet.

The Theory of Lungs

Breathe, breathe the tunes of long songs found in the alphabet, the a's and the b's and the c's all consubstantiated in grand theories of how the moon came to be and how the sun may one day get tired and become a dead start. Rosaries of letters contorted into meanings that may mean nothing in the end, but for now they suffice to appease our fears and solitudes, becoming the gods or the prelude to the gods we want to know but may never, never know. Breathe, breathe those tunes from far away, stealing them from the wind, that current that brings them from the origins, from Syria and Iraq and Lebanon or those other lands of ancient Mesopotamia. It all started because we needed to count money, to sell goods to our neighbours or buy their own. We wanted to taste the bread and the wine of distant lands to satiate that thing that in us runs and chants and calls for more, always. It all started because we needed to count money, money runs everything, that's what we think, but maybe it is not. Maybe it is not money that runs everything—maybe it is much deeper than that. Breathe, breathe in the long spaces that tell you how to live, revealing this thing that we call life, day in and day out, from the moment we get up, confused and dazed by the other world, throughout the day, all convoluted and contorted into the thing that we were not meant to be. Do not follow the blind, tumultuous labyrinth that takes you away from yourself from dawn to dusk, like a machine without soul. Embrace the higher order of things that call from within you, that you are, that are you. Break the letter of this stifled, dead alphabet that's wrapped itself around your beautiful neck. Make a singing rosary and create, sing to another God.

Notions of God

There are truly beautiful people in the world. And when they are truly beautiful, they remind you of God. They are God. And then you want to go on living in the world. In this world. Forever.

She dreamed of a Pegasus: a sturdy, gentle white horse with wings that would cross her from here to the end of the world, that would dance her into a round interminable whirl when she could finally be whole, nothing missing, accompanied by all. Feel the exact point. That would be her voyage to God. That would be God.

Between the point of her chest, where purple gulfs of life are executed impeccably by jinn from regions in superior Abyssinia, and the lower back of her spine, where marrow meets bone, she could spend whole days, immersed into things, true, full things, and feel as if all that ever was or would be, had joined her for a solemn session of precise collective understanding. Between those points and in those correct days, she sworn in frank and sincere faith, that her meeting had been with God.

Sometimes the valleys and the hills merged, and she could only know the world through encrypted notes, sounds that only people who don't speak any language know to be of very high value. It happened on special days when she chose to crisscross time without the thick sheet separating all the geometric figures that mark up the world, when she meandered between hopes and the ropes of minimal possibility, laying down her body fully on the earth. It was a darling pleasant game brought about by the deep nobility that drove her ontological desire, that inescapable fever always boiling in her blood. The red crimson lust of the voice that never left her, incessantly calling her to enter a better house: that coveted sleep into the dome of darkness or the castle of blind insight, depending on the alphabet you choose to name your prophet.

Waiting: It Is Pure Love

In the impossibility of the moment, hold on to the scent of the unknown and its fear. There may be something there: to be grasped with all the fingers of your tremulous hand. If you run away, the secret may never be caught by your open receiving palm where lines, still unfinished, are waiting, in ethereal attendance, to realize the way to the third moon of the brilliant Map. Waiting is pure love: for the things that you have not yet seen but to which you devote time every day, when the doubt arrives at your bones, cracking the fragile node of your bending knees making you fall or almost fall on the street of the hard world. You devote time, your time, in candid expectation so that the calcium and the marrow that are there, will, one day, unexpectedly, make your body a full, known thing, your person suddenly apprehended. Waiting: it is pure love.

The Medical Book

Yesterday I woke up feeling pain
All over the ligaments that tie this thing that I am together
I thought that in order to satisfy myself that all my bones were in place
And still intact, I needed to consult the medical book
That wise tome that lists one by one, all the bones of this physical treaty that my body is

I opened the book on page one, where the main bone, the spine, is discussed at length
I read and read in awe and concentration about how I am what I am because of this bone
How I walk straight every day because of its strength, how I think thoughts of love and hate
Because my spinal cord connects my body to my mind, my physical veins to the invisible, yet astounding soul of my cranium, without which I cannot exit the smallness of what I am

After this studied examination of my main pillar and the conductive lines that make me a sacred marionette, I turned the page to know more details about this thing that I am, this body that makes me be

At each turn I marveled at the specificity, the intricacy of each part of me
The little bones of each finger all tied to one another and then to the hand and then to the arm
Little boys and girls all working hard and in symphony to please the woman that I am and the goddess that I aspire to be

I am a thing made of many things, many bones, curves and counter-curves, blood that travels fast and deep keeping me sane and satiated and able to exhale and inhale the air of the spring and the cool breeze of the day, after the suffocating heat of an overly passionate and irrational summer

I have a heart that loves by pounding blood into myself reminding me of my responsibility to be kind to the world, to pour my own love in a cup and extend it to the lonely man and woman on the street with vacant, needy eyes—and hands that reach out

I have limbs and limbs, lymph node after lymph node, and kidneys that cleanse the debris in me so that I can then go out into the world and help in the sweeping of the streets making our place a temple where we can live (or at least survive better) and grow mature

I have all this in me, this alphabet of alphabets so that I can write off the bad moments and commence anew each day, enter the world in full capacity and hope, my feet touching the ground softly with full intent and innocent concern

I am a patient, perpetually regenerating language that fully believes in the capacity of verbs that then become nouns and all the other syntactic miracles of our loving human alphabet

I am a medical miracle, a medical tome engendered by the things that we do
The things that we do together and those that we do to one another and to ourselves

My Toenails

My toenails are growing too rapidly
I cut them every day: I want to walk unimpeded
By my own clumsiness
And look self-assured, neat—easy to the eye
Of men I am (still) trying to impress

My sandals are sexy: they have holes and straps
I dance with them, bouncing to the rhythm of my body
This cave that holds me down
Even when I want to suppress the jargon of everyday rubbish
And scribble a new clean alphabet
Through the spectacular ink that rivers my starved lymph nodes

Small Words

I told myself last night that I would, from now on,
Write short poems, ephemeral words here and there
Where life or the hint of its intractable sense could be figured out
Incanted in small doses to find body and house

I told myself this promise
Write small words, senseless lists that my intrinsic Lusitanian
taste
Bred on the other side of the Atlantic, with lush, emotional,
visceral sentences
Naturally rejects
Avid that it is to spew ink through nothingness and appease the
fear
And loneliness of life—that *fado* that we cannot escape

Go against that inclination, be the other of yourself
And in that process, find the twin that walks in you
And makes sense of you
You are, after all, a citizen of the world
And adaptation and growth are your ontological destiny

The Kitchen

The kitchen where she stands is bound to nothingness
In the middle there is the table
The bread and the olive oil, and on special days, a note of
rosemary
Singing its perfume amidst the stale air of condiments
Suspending the hard labour that the mistress of the house
endures

If I stare at the table long enough, I see all the people she has fed
Over the centuries, in aprons of colours entangled in grease stops
All marks of life, days and nights come and still your place
remains
The same corner is your corner

Dreams, you say,
Dreams are made of incense smells that I conjure in this small
corner
Where I live
Dreams are built from inside out

Perhaps she is right,
And I am only intruding on her perfection

A Dreamed Grammar

There is a grammar that keeps me down
I read it carefully
Obey all its commas and full stops
Breaking myself in halves constantly
Convoluting my intended ideal
Even if what I want is to be a full unbroken thing
A brown or white egg
Beautiful and stunning just like the mother hen intended
After her hard labour

One day I'll be able to fully un-write this grammar of millennia
Incomplete and contorted
And commence a treaty of true love
Wearing sandals that make me walk for my own sake
I'll forget what you did to me
Forget what men like you do to us and themselves
And move on to a new clean sphere
A true treaty of love
Feeling that wind that moves and kisses you on its way
To the intended way of being

One day, I'll summon the courage to recover
My oval perfection
A new A and a new Z
And all the words that can be composed in-between
That fabulous empty space
Waiting to be written in love, by love
My ideal no longer convoluted
Or confused by the rhetoric that kills

A Thing with the Hands

She has a thing about her hands
With her hands
They come and go incessantly
One child after the other, creating,
Controlling the world

Candles, lunar, insatiable for light
Searching through the night
And even in the light of the day
As if blind they were, these children of five legs each

She stares at them, straightens them
Long roads ahead of her
Showing her the things that she ought to become
Her internal drive always clocking her

She then raises her head and her eyes become
Infinite trains where the existential scar is continually eating
itself
At itself—a knife that you file even in your sleep in metaphors of
being
Conjured in the psychotic ramblings of the unborn

I watch her from afar
Want to tell her that she ought to control the impulse
For, like the dog, she can never bite her own tail
But then I let it be, let her be
For really there is no avail
To this story that writes us all
This hand of God that demands
It is the curse of Cain

Ambitious Cells

She recoiled into her cells,
Those ambitious membranes
That come alive when you least expect
And make you jump out of your bed
Fresh, incendiary, the fever of life
Pulsating all over her
As if all the spring light had suddenly
Entered her every bone
Making her dunk, drunk to the core
Her marrow leaking out of her
Radiating in the grand and magnanimous wave
That was the world
She is not a small thing
Never was

Love

Love is the longest word,
One that goes on from my own marrow to yours
Leaking our sorrows into one single bucket
Our beings joined in a single eternal woe
Polished by the stroke of two hearts

Love is vowel after vowel after vowel
Consonant after consonant
Each letter speaking feelings that surpass
What each manages to conjure

Between each letter of this long verb
(for love is "to do" onto others and yourself)
There lies the immensity of the pulse
That I am trying to tell you about
In the poverty of my grammar
For I am a mere mortal
Lonely shepherd of endless planes

Life

To live should be simple
It is in fact simple
When we walk straight every day
And look at the world before us
No condemnation, take it as it is
But make sure you do your part
Be kind, do not abuse
Walk straight, always, look people in the eye
As a promise that your word is real, will become real
Paved in concrete actions that build

Pick up dirty leaves when they stare at you
In them you may foresee the life of your own death
The beautiful ink of your own body now reborn
Into the humus of our astonishing land
That bed that always remembers to give birth to a new story
So that we know where we came from
And understand the responsibility to be kind

You—

I've called you inside me, deep in the furrows of my amber skin
With white open vowels from the Portuguese and English
alphabets
That dance in me and sing letters of a future
I noted all the wide sounds and the endless concave caves
Those spaces where being can be stretched to unlimited planes
And I saw the lilies of the valley and the grass petals in the
morning
Sitting in love, waiting for the gentle sun to come and soak them up
Diffused love, sprinkled back, like gentle kissing rain
In the rays of vernacular light

And you come in with liquid hands and clean smiles
You swim in me and I in you
We become the things that are meant to be,
That the world constantly calls for with its urgent cry for things,
Real things to be made
I've called you inside me, and you called me inside you,
My hand clean, holding onto your poles

We swam, stayed in the beautiful river
And adored the gaps of the babies to be born
You allowed me to speak in songs uttered in the moment,
Born out of a warm water of creation
I woke up with you in my face,
My hands certain that I was myself and that I was not alone
Two different streams, both needed to find the sea,
The wholeness that drives us all

I went to the horizon at sunset and sunrise,
Knelt down and prayed to your inner clean lagoon
At night I climbed into our made bed and passed you my rosary,
Imbedded in carnations and hydrangeas, laurels of the old
country
The petals of my Bible
Circulating in each of your limbs, creating hymns that enchant
the sturdiest atheists
For to live is to follow belief—that patience that calls

I was drunk with pure wine and I collided with the moons of the
cosmos
To be united
In the primal, primal thing, that is called you and I and all the rest

And then one day, I looked at you and you had disappeared
Perhaps had never been there, and I a lunatic of an unfound
universe
Imagined the twinkles in your eyes and the dimples in your
childish face
There are things we do not do to Love
Must never do
To ourselves
To others

Expansion

I have a tree in me, it can stagnate, it can flow outward, I becoming
the wind, seeing the galaxy, limbs spread, dipping into the ocean,
drinking the fish and the flesh of the flowers and startled stars that
sweep that dark luminous space, another abode of the sky above,
that we are all afraid of. But there is light, love there, bright candles
that see and take you out of the Calvary that you cross alone, day
in and day out, in this modernity of the capital you live in, inside
global cities where overly and obsessive individualized liberties
tell us we can all be what we want to be. Yes, we can, we can swim
in synchronized eternities on that superb flying floral carpet of
nothingness when the word in us expands, becoming the pure
children of God. I have a tree in me—it can stagnate like dead water
or fly outward, a fully living consummating mechanism, limbs
sprawled like a cat in a loving mood, I becoming the wind . . . I
forget, I love, I am born, reborn into decolonization, stretching the
word and the world it promises beyond the strong stubborn roots
that it has taken, destroying the magnanimous belly of the earth
and making us cry in front of a disgrace of our own making. Like
that general in South Africa, inside that beautiful book, reminding
us, his finger pointed at the disgraceful camps of inhumanity
created by men and women (us), screaming: "Look at this, take
a good look at this. This thing that we did!" The towers are our
towers, we make them. But I can meet you, us, them, escalating up
Mount Everest, and there on top we breathe, cold, fresh, refreshing
beings, new angles between earth and sky suddenly shown to
us—all is in me and you, our bone marrow leaking into blood and
water and the soup that we share. The Syrians are in all of us, give
them your house, place your bread and your wine on a large table:
bring olive oil for the senses. The circle where the sacred family
gathers—I am them, they are me—"us" we are.

Muttering Syllables

She lives alone in a house full of shadows
In her dwelling space the curtains are always semi-drawn
Not too much light, not too much darkness
Just the right dose of filtered rays (from the sun or the moon or
the stars)

She walks in this space morning to night in slow compassed
footsteps
Her feet enveloped in slippers made of dark cottons held together
by brown linen
And vines that have gone mature, and are now a deep, dark green
In the echoes of silence that she produces with this careful
movement of adorned feet
There lies a god that is humble, his head shaved, his beard clean
She sees him staring at her in the middle of the semi-illuminated
sphere of her dwellings
And she is taken by a sudden deluge of tenderness—a love spread
over her entire being,
Her entire house, the country where her house is located, then all
the other countries and also
The spaces and things that exist beyond all of that

She sees the word L-O-V-E splattered, spattered on everything
Spaces and objects become nothing and everything, convulsed,
confused
Abandoned gestures of the great Pangea—before the continents
broke down and loneliness
And race, and nationality and men and women were invented

Sometimes I peek into her isolated, recondite existence and I
marvel at her capacities
I want to be like her: I dream of being like her
And so I observe, in awe, hidden in my spot of immature pupil
that wants to be, to become more

My sole objective, in the course of my life, is to absorb something
from her and from the god she listens to—the god with a small
"g" who has a shaved head and beard clean
And so I stare at her in wonder, when I have time and am freed
from the businesses of everyday life

In good days and when I am really paying attention and stay long
enough,
I can feel the lesson coming to me
In precious muttering syllables—words that are beyond words
Things that have a body and a soul, and which I can see, smell
and touch and feel
Living scripts entering my blood, my plasma, my wounds

In those moments, I have a glimpse of true life, my ontological
vacuum suddenly filled
With the every-thingness that we are and want to be
My oxygenated lungs breathe fully—and in that mere moment
life becomes eternal
My broken self suddenly suspended and filled to capacity
I know then that this body of life is my destiny

Mãe

My mother calls me at night, with varicose veins and inflated body that can barely move. Her boys went to war and she struggled to make sense of it all. She carried herself stoutly in the face of this life that can be so unkind. And there were children, so many of them, demanding bread and water. The soup of God too. Liquid and clean, washing you to the valleys of cosmic wonders. Dreams struggling to emerge out of the nothingness of those rocky harsh mountains of Beira Alta. So many dreams, mom: riddles to be solved and show the beautiful poem that life is—or ought to be. The stunning alphabet of our existential yearning, dripping slowly like the tears of morning dew, still fresh from a night that was full.

Broken Down: Make Me Whole

There is an obsession with portraying an important, successful and happy life online: with perfect photos, tall elegant glasses of wine alongside toes painted red, sexy-sexy, side by side with "important" people or statues of important people apparently doing impressive things for the world. Attending concerts inside Leonardo da Vinci's potent and overly decorated opera house, somewhere in the beautiful capital of some ex-Roman empire that yearns to gain the luster and power of bygone days when it thought itself king of (and kind to) the world (empires tend to do that). Because we all need heroes—but what kind of heroes? Pretty dogs with perfectly groomed hair or running wild in the wild in some nice North-American farm that used to belong to another people. Oysters and half lemons in the shape of half-moons on a perfectly set table for two, alluring us in to the mystical that we lack and can't quite find on this bloody carnivorous earth of ours where we eat one another all the time without any scruples, despite the image. The image is everything. Statements of presidents or smiles of presidents or their immediate aids aiding us and our cause in immaculately conceived rhetoric that has gone way beyond Aristotle's initial (and already pretty sordid) conjecture about our human (in) capacities. And the list goes on ad infinitum. PS. Did you know that da Vinci was the son of a poor peasant young woman (and an upper-class man) who then became a genius capable of thickening the ligaments between the left and the right side of the brain so that he could REALLY see? True fact: he hated dichotomies and yearned to be whole.

Celebrating

Carnations. Red. Beautiful. They grow in the soul of those who
dream freedom and justice. Celebrating Portugal's Carnation
Revolution (25 of April, 1974) when the military, through a fairly
peaceful coup turned against fascism, the colonial wars, and
decided to put carnations in the barrels of their guns to burn the
hate. I was almost 5 years old. I must remember: the colours and
images, the vibrancy of a special spring waking up the tormented
earth, the songs, the hope, the mailman singing and blowing
his horn to announce the arrival of a true new letter . . . Not like
the others with dark mourning stripes. The dreams eager to see
the light of the morning and then walk through the day like tall
stunning things that have legs and hands that clean the world
and erect sturdy cities where we all find shelter . . . Suffocated
yearnings suddenly erupting from people's throats with that
raw incandescent enthusiasm and beauty that children possess,
shouting "Viva a Liberdade!" The mothers of those men-boys
down south destroying and being destroyed, now singing a gay
alleluia, breathing deep and laughing at the core. Brothers A and
Z were coming home. *Viva a Liberdade. Viva o amor.* Carnations
are red: read them. Carnations and read and beautiful. The colour
of the sunrise. A blood of love.

The Mornings

They come to you
announcing existence each day with an insistence
that calls, begs for patience

You may want to feel sorry and sad and give it all up
because this thing, nebulous, painful, impossible to take
is always there, in its strangeness, in its calling, its mute voice
your mind does not know how to apprehend it
how to make it ordained and neat
drawn in the line that you want it to be

You may insist on staying in bed wishing that you forget it all
and then wake up one day when all is clarified
and you feel new and able to find out all about it,
its mysteries and sagas explained by the godly philosopher
who has access to it all, the circuitous node finally unveiled

But the mornings are always yours and you alone can unclutter
the vision that you see in the short window of your horizon
do not cry, child, for a small god who is blind
do not cry child, for that god lives inside your own house
call it, using all the songs that I know play inside you
because "music is movement that cannot be seen"
someone once said

Do not stay in bed all day
step out slowly—even if it's hard
in that slowness let your feet find floor on the amber brown wood
that cements your mansion
firm your intentions like a new born human

who dreamed about a life that can be fashioned
and where children and fountains and valleys
are all toys that know the way to the river that washes clean
under the shadow of a moon that though in midcycle
is walking to the destiny of its fullness

She Keeps Falling

She keeps falling in love
For the Os and the As and all the others that she senses inhabit
our long musical alphabet
Those men with deep voices and poetic undertones, lonely like
her, even if they deny it
Still putting on the thick mask of masculinity: the tie and the
muscle, the MBAs or the Ivy League schools they attended or
have taught at

She falls and falls in love with them, for them
The Os and the As and all the other men that meander in the
lonely lines of our long alphabet
Lost in the vacuous nights of existence, when the wives, tired
and worn down are asleep, and the children dream innocently,
sucking their fingers, immersed in the bliss of wholeness

She keeps falling in love
For the Os and the As and all the others that she senses inhabit
our long musical alphabet
Men with deep voices and poetic undertones
Most of whom she has never even seen
Only connecting with them sporadically through the
inconsistency of the cybernetic waves
Pulled by a magnetism, that current akin to the eternal loving,
longing soul that travels far and deep, that part of us that yearns
and yearns searching for the face of the beloved in the
Gardens of the city, like the Buddhist therapist says in his wise
book to us

Us, all lost in this thick citadel that we have created with our
superb technology
Another tool to erase or suspend the loneliness that never seems
to go away
Leaving us consistently broken, incendiary tears in our sad eyes,
ready to leave the orbits
And cry our fragility into the concrete streets of the world
Our beautiful eyes—those deep, deep pools that call
Call for something that may not in fact exist, and which we,
stubborn beasts
Of existence, eternal dwellers of the ontological vacuum, keep
trying to uncover

She keeps falling in love
For the Os and the As—those open circular letters that never end
Men with poetic voices and deep undertones
That make you feel infinite, your body expanded in chants and
hymns
Convulsion and convulsions only imagined in the long lonely
nights of her large bed

She falls and falls in love with them, for them
The instrument forever singing all and everything that exists and
ever existed
Travelling between waves, magna among magna, the dream of
God's song
Or God itself—until she falls asleep alone

The Economics of Linguistic Exchange

The con artists of our time dress and speak well. They move to the right neighbourhood and often even work for good, powerful institutions hiding behind their suits and never get caught or fired. But if you dress and speak like a beggar or a peasant, society is blind to you: you are just a beggar or a peasant and it is unlikely that you can "move to the right neighbourhood." But at least you are what you are: proud copy of your own self without the lie of the veneer. You speak your alphabet, true letters uttered in stutters, forced out of your convulsed, convoluted body that bends down day in and day out: an honest labourer with no pretension to the throne. Like my darling grandmother, who had two daughters out of wedlock and a clean house up on the mountain village, where electricity reached late. Her eyes were always clear and blue. I remember. The symbolic powers of speech, dress and location . . . Pierre Bourdieu, the Frenchman was quite right.

This Love, This Light

Bring me the shadows of your self
Under that kind, soft, insecure light
Where I can dream what you are and decode
All the lymph nodes of your body
Stare at your poetic undertones
The languid calmness of the world
Before my hands and my eyes
A sanctuary for meditation

Bring me the light-dark luminous candor of the thing
That in you murmurs and dreams and loves
Do not show your full self under the crude light of the day
In midsummer when dreams have no space to be detected
Blind that they are by the splendor of rational shortcomings
Come slowly, in nights clean, at dusk or dawn
When the freshness and incantations of the cosmos
Sing eternally through the porous lines that surround your figure

Bring yourself in cadent, slow moments and movements
Without the harshness of the speedy and the bluntness of the
luminous
That affect those days without shadow
Be kind to the mystery that you are: seduce me peacefully,
gradually, gracefully
In languid undertones of browns and blacks and greys
The rainbows where dream nests
That mysterious, mystic house where I find myself and you
It is this love that I crave
This light
This possibility

Charcoal-Burning

When I was a very young girl, I used to go with my mother to make charcoal in the forest or in the lands around the village. My mother, who could do almost any job that life demanded from her: and life demanded a lot from her. That ought to be pure poetry in the bone. "Charcoal is a beautiful thing to turn out, when your kiln is burnt and opened up, and the contents spread on the ground" like that lyrical woman said, the one who wrote (Africa) Out of Africa. Perhaps she was mourning, deeply inside her, the fantasy of her own wild, endless, whole landscape, recalling in what she saw on the continent, what she herself was missing in her, had forgotten how to make live—perhaps she was not really a racist and all she really craved was to merge with the other, to be more with her Self. We all do this, this way or another way. We forge mirages in hopes of filling the space that never seems to be filled, always hungry for something it does not even know how to name: the poetry in the bone. Or the kiln of the plant once it's clean and light: black as a pearl, pure to the marrow. It is then that we may be able to take to the skies.

The Being in Being

There is beauty and fragility
and also grandness and greatness,
in being a being of the universe.

In your smallness, and if you wish,
you could hold it with your own finger,
the universe that is.

And then you would no longer know
whether it is the universe holding you
or you holding it in you.

Today, This Morning

Today, this morning, I am blooming in white: white is the blooming, glorious colour of my nascent spirit which I have kept underground, in winters cold and long, hidden in the limbs of a child that within me tries to walk into a real pulsating time. Outside the night of my doom, when I was cloaked in skimpy clothes, hibernated in useless thoughts of your dark smooth hands that promised me the eternal flower of the wind, when night and day, moon and sun join in the hug of priestly sermons and we forgive and forget, only to be, to love more. Your dark hands that never came. Today, this morning, I am blooming in white, I am the bride of the morning dawn and the azure of the endless vacuum that I see at night when I go outside and dance under the abracadabra of the possibility of a vacant air.

Desire

Deep below the curtains of the marshlands
She holds a desire: fly even below to meet the syncopated sounds
Of the smallest beasts and worms, the primary agents of this
upper crust
Where we live and think we command life and civilization

Her desire is so visceral that she spends days and nights, even
months
Without a break, obsessed with this expedition, this pulse of the
pulse
That makes her blood redder and her invisible legs somersault in
avid gulfs
Of tepid or dark air

If you observe her from afar, you may note how this intangible
need of hers
Consumes her life, and then realize the eventless meander of
your own days
Because you are not yourself possessed by any such gut cause, any
primary reason
And then, if your pride does not take over the insight of the
moment and you see
Yourself as a road unfinished but willing to try the paths of
different curves
You may come to a grand finding, your ontological desire
suddenly reawakened

I Am Preparing Myself

I am preparing myself for the big event.
I will emerge out of my skin unafraid and walk in silky feet
toward the world to find a real "being" that will allow me
to become and who will become with me.

I am made of cherries and peaches: delicate succulent fruits that
give water to the needy.
My poetic line obeys many commands: the full stops and the
commas come sporadically and only when the vibration of the
other pulls inward.

I am preparing myself for the big event.
My silky feet meandering the curves of your body, the cells and
subcells of that space that lives in the arched cave of your wonder
valley.

My Self is not a mute stone: it arcs toward the language that the
other speaks.
That sweet tongue that will extend my bones and their marrow
making me everlasting.
The satiated lioness of the prairies at the altar of everything.
A flying bird, transparent, transposing, transposed.

Our Matter

Our matter matters.
It is made of dreams.
From the cells to the subcells to the liquid of the bone marrow.
And the dreams spread into broad, thick green leaves.
And in its nest, there are red fruits bearing the attitude of life.
Let them grow this time and every day after.

Sometimes I Don't Know

Sometimes I don't know. I don't know because that's just the nature of life: we don't know. We just don't know. As simple as that. The problem is that we have to sound as if we know—as if we got a profound and right answer for everything even if our answer is full of doubt, words and verbs that attack one another like rival hungry enemies of the worst kind that insist on trashing the castle we want to build, if only to house enemies to our future fulfillment. Call it the logic of the fool—or the logic of fear. Induced by immature existentialists or greedy capitalists out to make a buck from human misery. But the truth, the real truth is that sometimes we just don't know and so it is better to just say nothing: to stay in the vacuous cavernous music of nothingness, the place of unspoken words when the black cat is asleep and you can only remember his open eyes as very slight speckles of light. Stay there and face the emptiness of your own certainties. It is better because that is honesty—that action without pretense: weak but pure, weak but real. And to be human is always better than anything else, better than to be super-human or sub-human. To be human is to kneel down before the scantiness of life. And not be ashamed of doing so. Even when the king is looking at you and you know that your next meal may be cut off.

Learning Love

She learned to like men who care: really care. Not those who step
on you and use you as a ladder to build their ego, not knowing
that that vulnerable part of ourselves can never be satisfied, will
always crumble, raging from passion to passion and consuming
others and itself in the process. She learned to love men who
are human beings, humble, in a process of growth, who push
themselves through a process of elevation, hard and confusing as
it may be, while quite aware that they are not gods but do have
that sacred and fiery potential in them. And she learned how to
love women who do the same. She learned how to love herself.
She was a thing in movement and ontological fulfillment was her
final destiny.

Lines of Something

On a day like that there was only one thing to do: have a conversation about cold and love. And the loneliness that our bare existence is. We may have created metallic lines, sturdy and elongated with the intent to become immortal, vain that we are, or just merely afraid. We may have thought to have amassed thick layers of importance and grandiosity, throwing parties for ourselves, inhabiting a deluded world of pomp invented in a state of myopic euphoria when the vast geography in front of our eyes is erased, but in the end, in cold and lonely days, when our lovers have all abandoned us, we cannot think but of the sorrow that we have caused to one another and to ourselves: how we failed to see beyond the small corner of our house to meet the vast extension that life is, construct arcs of humanity, the only ones that make us into something that really matters. Beautiful lines of something.

Resistance

You can beat me out of shape with your heavy merciless, pounding hammer, that machine of money and illusions. Tall orders and ties and public fake profiles that you throw around and live by. That hand of yours that seems pure but is not. You can beat me up. Yet I shall always remain pure, swimming in my sacred rivers, below the dirty crust, where the marrow is dancing to build life that is. The incessant obsession without which there can be no love. Pure, true love—clean like the sparkle of the girlish eye, between hay and open field. Open like air and sky and sea. You can bend me down and twist my limbs until I become a shapeless well of nothingness but I shall always recover, recoiled in my dreams of lucidity, where not even you, despite your strength and the many hands that give you life, can muddle my naturally clean body. And when I am down on my luck, my spirit tired by the living times that sing odes to the dirty kings and queens, when I am down on my luck, ridden with the sorrows of the dejected hopes of the millions of beings of this world and the one beyond, I shall still find courage. To bathe in the undercurrents of rivers not yet contaminated by you or with water carried in the ceramic pots from the fountain I used to drink in. When I was a child in that eternal village of people huddled together to live decently under the pressures of a greedy dictator, who, born in the landless peasantry, a serf to the core, deep down suffered from a great complex of inferiority. As Fanon said, in a fatalist illogic logic, the oppressed often wants to press others down using the same iron that was used to chain him. Instead of choosing to break the cord, which he could break if he really wanted, he prefers to climb the table and find a place on top of the tower. Do not twist my limbs, beast of the iron machine. Do not, for there lives in me a circular cavernous grace that never forgets what it is to be, to live—and look, unburdened, at the power of the laughing sun.

To Feel or Not to Feel

If, on any given day, you wake up fully conscious, feeling all the weight of the world, you won't be able to withstand it. The good thing is that God, or what passes for it, can make you numb. Though there are, of course, dangers associated with this numbness. Very great dangers, dangers that create more and more weight for you to feel and so it is hard to know how one should wake up every morning and go about the day.

There Are No Words

There are no words. If there were words, I would see their salt and light and bright yellow cooper temper me with the eternal lingering of a scintillating life. There are no words: you babble them out in a semi-awakened state putting your feet where your mouth is, playing dangerous, deadly games with the soul. Not just yours, but ours too, for how can the eagle fly alone and build mansions in the faraway land without the aiding rope that you put out? There are no words: you babble them out, entangled that you are in the corporate game of the land whose rhetoric Socrates and Aristotle had warned us about long time ago—and before them, many others. There are no words: the ears have gone blind. And then you go to sleep and the flying dreams don't come: you are stuck to the piercing fence by the low land, your body incarcerated, incapable of dancing through the universe, unable to fulfill its destiny, your destiny, our destiny. There are no words. What saves you then?

The Love of Sunday

When she reaches the goal of Sunday love, without the passion that rips up her insides, lacerating the moist thing she is made of, his voice and skin will no longer intrude in the ancient sepia colours of her true self. Her nodules will finally be cleared, cleansed. Delivered she will be. The cancer will die: no longer fed by the malignant confused cell that does not know when enough is enough and keeps spewing out matter that does not matter. Killing in the name of an uncalled for grandeur.

Spirals of Laughter and Being

The sun comes up dripping spring and breathing light into the incessant falling tears of your sorrow. The earth is clear and the spiral clenches of mesmerizing magics that renew and forget and forgive, licking you up and down. You live and walk and see: free and unencumbered for a day, for an hour, for a minute, and in that sentience, that sense, that sensibility, that sentence, the world is eternal, magnificent, the magnanimous revelation that tells you who you are. You are clean, you are whole, a person of this earth, born naked, born ready, born capable. On this day. Spirals of laughter and being.

When You Write a Letter

When you write a letter, write it well. The words that you ink will tell (and do) something. Do the same with a note: even if you are in a hurry, or anxious about what you are saying, what you mean to say, for whatever reason. And when you speak, follow the same pattern. Words are patterns that leave, forge marks on the floor we all walk in. If the words fail, we fail, we fall on the floor of nothingness, bleeding from the knees.

The Darling Language

I shall look at you in the eye and not blink, not think that I am the one at fault, not allow your supposedly cool ways to shatter my inner integrity, the darling love for myself. I shall not let the dark race of fear and humiliation make my heart pump like that of the strayed child who has lost the hand of her mother at the crazy carnival where the clowns have macabre tricky faces that confuse you to the core. I shall not be that lamb running from the wolf who has dressed himself as a sheep. I shall walk with my shoulders straight, my feet firmly stepping on the ground, proud of my mother, my father, all the limbs and veins that run through me. And the tears and the screams too—the only language I can speak when the time is endless and there seems to be no hope for love. That darling language that we seldom manage to speak.

Advice to the Lost

When you enter the world, enter it slowly and with grace
Every day dance candidly
to the tune of the music playing in your soul.
Do not step onto others,
those who over and over again open a line for you to get your chance
and clarify your existential turmoil.

For the Love of Words

Nothing as soothing as being in and with words. They take you away and bring you back to yourself, only more so. You become a Self because you travel through the meanderings of all the peoples' lives, anchored in these diaphanous, porous and yet relentless floors of astonishing beingness. Peoples of the entire world, all of them. You see them. You pause and think between words, peeking at their visions, their sufferings, their awes, entering the line that has no end. You find yourself in them and through them . . . The words are the people and you. You are a line, aligned, with the same matter crawling upon your insides. You know you are part of a big beautiful thing that breeds and sings and bleeds together. The same wound. The same song. The same bread. The same house. Words make us eternal, chained to the same cause. They are body and profound spirit.

The Potential of Verbs

They do it because they can. They have done it because they
could. They will do it again if they can. Unless this form of
the verb (this verb "can") is suspended from our grammar for a
thorough examination which demands a conscientious personal
and collective "revolution", one that requires (pushes) the self
and the other to encounter each other in truly genuine ways.
Which can be done. And then the verb "can" would really mean
something. There is a pearl at the bottom of the ocean waiting to
be found—a can of marvels yearning to be unpacked by our sorry
souls. We can, said the politician. Blessed be "he."

The Thing Lingering in Me

The soft feeling of that thing, that love that I felt for you still lingers around all the corners of all my being sometimes, membranes and membranes of unclosed molecules that wait for the missing protons. Yes, it still lingers, waiting in an unending erect pose. Especially on really dark days when sorrow and loneliness cry out and I think about the very fundamental things of life. This life, which we were given to make into something astounding and vibrating, like air circulating pure in the form of a smile, or a clear moon, or a child's waving laughter in my eye. I think about you: why do such things to me? And so many times. To play a game of words: of I want you but I don't. A tease for the ego: yours. And I, a prey for that wolf that you have not been able to tame so it goes on ravaging the meat of others. And I, hopeful for beauty, and a lover of words, falling into it again and again. I linger in these old paradigms, of what I thought it was and still want it to be—at least to clear the waters so that the river inside can be clean again and can, certain and unencumbered, reach its sea. So I am putting it out there: if you can find it in you to tell me why, give me a real clean word. If you can cleanse me of this thing that you dirtied me with, I would be thankful. And I truly believe that it would be good for you too: for your body and for your soul. And the health of the universe: that cord so fragile.

This Is for You

My soul is searching within the dark channels that the world throws at me: wires of caves and concaves taking in all my desires, depleting my whole skin and the organs underneath, the organs that my progenitors created with so much care, so much love. And that my mother then engendered inside her, day after day, the heart, the liver, the lungs, the ears, the perfect angles of my nose and my slanted Euro-Asian eyes. Day after day, with so much care, so much patience. I have been wanting to write to you, about you, throw really harsh rocks at you this time. Because all the other times I was careful, so careful, walking on eggshells and afraid of the princess that I still want to believe is a heroine: despite all the evidence. But there is no lying anymore, there can be no lying anymore . . . The electrons of the alphabet that in me dwells have paralyzed in circular and sick motions in my head, my sacred cranium failing to resolve the deep injuries of all my vocal cords, those that crave for universal, whole music. But the true alphabet is calling me—an invitation that I really need to take in and practice like a saint—to attain sanity, sanctity, sanity. And let you go. Let you go.

Mantles

Cover me up with skin, your dead and living cells
Those meandering through all the surfaces of your body
Each limb, each finger, the space in your belly,
and the masculinity below it—that cave concave
that makes me disappear sometimes and dream of lions flying in
savannahs full of hay, gliding to the non-world

Cover me with your skin, dead and live cells
I want to see how you taste when alive and then dead
So that I won't even miss you when you are gone
And I am left resting in the aftermath of another doomed love
affair

Come when I am asleep and dance with my aura,
That liquid shadow in colours that appears at night
That you can see dancing above me
So that all our substances,
The substantiated and unsubstantiated
Become real

Mantles
Made with the timid but persistent preoccupation
Of the needy and alone

Cover me with your skin, your dead and live cells
Approach me from every angle so that I can stare at your
ambivalence
And dwell in the significance of your specificities

Categories of Aloneness

She and he are darlings of the soul
So that is what they constantly tell themselves
They met very young—and they knew right away

That is the story that they always remind themselves
So afraid to forget they are
They believe in karma or destiny
Depending on the religion, those words are easily
interchangeable
and we find followers of this ditty, belief if you will, in every
corner of our earth

They (she and he) spend days alone and together convincing
themselves and each other
Of this unmoved veracity: their a priori, fundamental and
unchallengeable love
Sometimes so much time is devoted to this exercise, and in
arguments that range from the emotional to the intellectual, to
the spiritual to the hysterical, that they forget what they claim
unites them by destiny

I watch them from afar and recall the line my father always used
when observing similar circumstances: "They are like dogs trying
to bite their own tail"—silly dogs

Lucinda

Lucinda, Lucinda, Lucinda
is a woman

Standing at the corner of a street
She never told me her name but I ventured to guess her luminosity

She stands at the same corner on a street every day
When night comes and she can shine more because the sun, now
tired of our world,
retired into another
Or is perhaps just on a reflective philosophical break, trying to
sort out matters
matters important to the bone

She stands at the same corner on a street every day
When night comes and the sun has gone away

It is a trick of the profession she has had to learn aided by those
who came before her
Who taught her some necessary and fundamental trade tips
Women helping each other ever since the tide went against them,
putting shadows
on a skin that was initially conceived clean—despite the posterior
efforts of the religious rhetoricians, philosophers, the politicians,
the disciplinarians

You can see it (the clean skin: yours and hers) if you undo the
sheets and live in a house where you are allowed to read and write
and then write again and again—undoing yourself ad infinitum
Until you find the node—clean and fundamental that nothing
can sully

Lucinda is neither tall nor particularly pretty
She is neither strong nor particularly weak
She is what she is or she is what she has been made to be

Lucinda, Lucinda, Lucinda
is a woman

And her name vibrates with the powers she is trying to recapture

Ana's Body

In her dream, she was flying away
In a white, open, silk skirt, moving steadily from the earth's
sphere
The more she flew away the better she felt
There were no heavy chains pulling her body to the eyes of
vultures
Her breasts were sacred magnificent mouths
Opening orifices of the earth freely giving milk to the needy

In her dream, Ana felt closer to herself than ever, and also close to
all and everything
There were no fingers pulling her down or eyes of vultures that
xerox your insights
Unashamedly thinking they can know all that you are
In her flying dream,
She was the Madonna of all times, before the era of Christ
And all the stories of Abraham the Patriarch that gave birth to
many religions
She was the true Virgin whose sacred body she chose to give to
the needy creatures
Out of pure and candid affiliation with her human fellows
That string that unites them since the big bang

She was a body of joy
Finally encountering her ontological destiny
She was free—she was Ana
In search of what it is she was born to do—and be

How Much Love

How much love do you have
to give to the beggar in the street?
to the street looking gloomy
full of little girls and cigarette butts
teens under attack by pimps and their network comrades?

How much science does your smile need
to watch with objectivity the lines on the faces
that run into you
eyes small, barely illuminated by the glory of the stars?
to grasp the marks on the floor where a passerby got on his knees
before closing his heart to the life of this world?

How much stare do you allow yourself
to the immaculate spot that is the woman beside you
who has spent days preparing her face for the world
so that people like you can actually see her?

How much love do you give to yourself
at night before you go to bed
or in the morning when the body cries to stay in
but your children call you from above for there is bread to be
made?

How much patience do you ask your bones to have
and all the muscles that help you run and breathe and open
your vocal cords to sing the marvelous force that in you dwells
when all the memories of that love haunt you to the bone and
make you doubt
that thing that in you is always sacred?

How much love
have you felt since you were born
but then had to hide its brilliance because
there are rules to play by?

How much love

I Do Not Speak

I do not speak in the original
I speak an adulterated language
That you passed on to me
You—who are also a fake,
Mumbling syllables that do not tell the truth,
the whole truth and nothing but the truth

I speak things that you and the world passed on to me
Scrappers that you all are
But I am not content with this charitable language
I dream and search for the tongue before I took in yours
Before you stole it from me when you gave me a hand and
Taught me your alphabet
And then syllables and words and sentences . . .

Before I knew I was mastering entire texts
Elaborate rhetorical schemes
Laws about the eternal and the universal
The earthly, the worthy and nonworthy
What a rose is what it is not
Why dogs are on the street
The local and the transnational
The Mexican and the Russian and the Nigerian
And the hypothetical creature on the Moon

I do not speak in the original
I spew a tongue infected by melanomas
Scientific and objective shortcomings that codify the mystery

I do not speak the original
Though I may occasionally, in distraction, enter the terrain
Of my *língua pura*
And babble ad infinitum

Until you wake me up
It is the night that saves me

Perhaps

Perhaps the truth about yourself is that little voice that whispers
and not the loud voices that shout and scream
perhaps the loud voices that shout and scream are just voicing
fears
from others

spit at you

their dreams or the dreams they have also heard from others . . .
perhaps the subtle little murmurs that come to you when you are
really alert
are the ones that truly speak and which you must listen to

perhaps

Space

She tries to fill the space that in her feels cavernous
Never-ending, open, dark, engulfing
She searches and searches for methods to do so

When travelling distances on airplanes
She takes the headphones, the self-help books
The magazines exploding with the exuberance of successful
people
The glasses to read the books or see the screen that entertains

When at the gym, taming down the body
She does pretty much the same
Dresses body with provoking clothes
And walks with singular elegance regulating her silhouette
And exposing with a large belt a tiny waist
The glories of being a modern, desirable woman

Before going to sleep, another space that in her aches
Tries to be filled
Moisturizers, slogans, codes to remember
Words evoked in her mind intimating to her
How much further she still needs to go
The circle in her eye (which ought to be clear) looks at itself
In the mirror and shakes, almost cries, asking for more
But she is not seeing its demands

She has filled all her empty spaces with tasks to accomplish
And she is so tired that life has become a parade of movements
Not a glory to be lived and truly felt
Not a horizon to decode slowly and peacefully
When drops of water bathe you and cleanse you to the bone

Sometimes when she is distracted and out of nowhere
A voice murmurs all over herself
(in the tiniest membranes that are still growing)

It tells her:

I want to feel what it is to be alive
Give me memory
And scintillating nebulous access to the stars
Make me caress the furs of a dog
The cactus on an imaginary desert
The aluminum cages that are not cages
For their light reverberates in circular
Unending waves that make me sink
Into all and everything
Inhabit light
That gives and gives
When I no longer feel any need to fill space
Because space is all that I am
And space is all that exists

When emptiness equates fullness

I Saw a Man Crying in the Street

I saw a tall man crying in the street
He was right there, in the middle of a busy street
His knees on the ground howling like a baby wolf

I saw him and I wanted to help him get up and so I crossed to his side
I looked him in the eye, between the translucent tears of his pain
I stood there waiting to be washed by his river
I asked him why was a man of his stature crying

At first he was silent but then looking at me with all that was left of his blurry eyes, between tears and pain, he said:

"I did not love her as I wanted to, as I should have,
as she dreamed she would be loved when she was a little girl;
I did not love her deeply enough, saintly enough,
with the profundity that true love requires. She was born for nothing;
to not know what total abandon is or loss of self in the other;
the 'he' that I am was born for nothing."

I felt deeply for him, for I saw in his story the one I had just lived, with that love of mine,
that beautiful love of mine, that had not been beautiful at all.
Though my story was slightly different for my love fooled me altogether; he put me right on my knees to receive what he had promised with magnificent metaphors freshly born from his lips, and then, then he ran away without a word, leaving me there, stranded, waiting like a begging saint, for the eternal, which would never come.

I told the tall crying man: "Maybe you can tell her still and make up for lost time."
He said: "It's too late. She died: will no longer believe."

I felt an immense sadness come over me: for this man, for myself, for his woman who had died, for my beautiful love, who left me hanging slowly, from the ropes of a promise, on my knees, his words nothing more than a cavernous echo that keeps playing within the empty fields that are my body and my soul, these sheets that see me wake up and go to sleep.

I knelt down to the tall crying man and I kissed him on the forehead. At least he had repented, a man manly enough to allow remorse for the vase he had broken.

And then I went home, and part of me, a stubborn believing part that does not want to die, knelt down like the tall crying man on the street, and started waiting for the eternal.

"For saints must have patience"—my mother told me when I was little.

Hiding

The particulars of my singularities are hidden from passengers
I sit near the rear of the streetcar hiding my nerves between the warmth
Of my purple gloves, inside disconnected synthetic fibers bought at Walmart
Where things are cheap and all workers have accents, newcomers to this land
One day we will understand them fully, their own plights enunciated clearly,
finally interceding with our own daily lives—brothers and sisters of a city,
the same city, when it's cold, in the dead of winter

I twitch and twitch in my invisible singular nest
I try not to look around where the screaming woman with pink hair
Is howling like crazy—that must be what she is: crazy
The streetcar is full
No one hears her and all try to sit on the opposite side of her
In infinite spaces as if the earth had no end and could not be measured in exact kilometers with our savvy scientific instruments
perfected by Einstein and all his companions

Her screams are becoming very hard to ignore
One person says: "shut up"
The driver, emboldened, adds:
"This is Queen Street, I am going to leave you here, if you don't stop."

I am still at the back, hiding my singularities from all passengers
of this life
My fingers whirling between my purple gloves, bought cheap at
Walmart
Where all the workers pronounce words in a singular way,
Though they are words like our words

I could join her—the crazy woman—but then they would know
That I too have singularities like the accents of the newcomers at
Walmart
So I stay anonymous, like all of us on the streetcar
Including the crazy woman—whom no one understands,
Convulsed that she is in her own odd humanity, trying to
convulse us too
But we are cowards, cowering down under the weight of what
our lives really are
We might as well die—for dead we are already
In a sameness that does not bulge

The Wise One

He is like Othello or the mind that made him be
A chronicler of people's complete existence
Their wounds, the most raw and open
Their awe for the sun with its brilliance and blinding spots
Their toes open to the wind in search of freedom
Their kneeling-downs and all its reasons

He is, like Othello or the mind that made him be
The diviner of moons and the other dead and living stars
Way beyond our firmament
His glasses endowed with scientific miracles
Not yet devised in our era

Like Othello
He is the poet of stars and stones and perfectly spread olive
orchards
In the Holy Land—where Lazarus fell ill, wounded by the
incurable
When God really existed and made lepers rise from death

How and Why and What?

Accept my words as they come. Do not mutilate them into a nothingness out of a need to feed a hole in you that has no borders. Accept them as my most profound way to communicate things that no words can ever tell, even when we extend them beyond their limits, like I try to do when I write these poetic inclinations that come to me. They come to me like obsessions, wounds sprung from existential enigmas, mysterious pains that lacerate all my nerves and tendons, bottom to top, top to bottom. I wish I had access to the language that God uses but never taught us. I wish he, God, did not make this miracle that our life is and then abandon us, making us lost children, sprung here and there, accidental life. Mere children, waiting for growth, meandering through the meadows that the seasons bring or the vacuums that the long afternoons deepen in our chests. They cry and scream to be fed with meaning: How do I know that life makes sense? How do I know that my nose is a nose? Is the name true to the thing? How do I shake the hands of a dying person and look that person in the eye while telling her, "everything is OK, everything will be OK." What is everything? How do I know that everything in fact exists and that existence is existing and not merely wanting to exist, like I try to here and now pushing words beyond reason and reasonable meaning? All but questions, questions, but no answers . . . And here we are, trying to be more, here we are dwelling on this earth, as for the rest, the beyond this here and now, we have no say at all, no knowledge at all . . . And so the fear just deepens. Forgetting everything and just being and living scantily and in awe may be what saves us then—what gives us access to all and everything. Because in the void, the brilliance of the imagination takes hold and your world become a paradise—a thing full to the rim. No more room to fill. That is bliss—said a poet I once read. Her name is a secret that only I have keys to decode. So please do not beg for the door to be opened. No. Do your own work.

A Fashionable Woman

She was a very special woman, the most special. He had never met anyone like her. Every time he met her, whether in the countryside or the city, in a recondite or open place, she showed up, as if on purpose, dressed in clothes that least favored her. And she did the same with the photos she put on Facebook: always the ones that showed the least attractive angle of her face, the most or least salient curve, always against the trend of the day. And he became more and more surprised, more and more fascinated with that naked woman, always unfashionable. That was her fashion. And it was this trend of hers that became an unbeatable love, his own fashion.

Words Calling

Words call me
I see a lonely word on a wall and I invent sisters and brothers
To play with her

I call Magda and Antonio and Ethan and Rose
And the circle commences

Words call me
I gaze at a commercial and I see "stunning"
And then everything happens
The white teeth of the woman become my dead grandmother
Who came to me in a night of long bad dreams and told me to
live my life
Informing me that she had forgotten my faults when caring for her
For I was only sixteen and could not do any better
And my mother, my mother was engaged in other tasks
Heavy loads weighing on her varicose veins

I look at the title of the conference imprinted on a sophisticated
power-point platform on the wall: "Real Conversations." I laugh in
silence because I know that we live in an overly politically correct
society that encourages no such thing—always enveloping the
shiny beauty in a sorrowful mantle that lies to protect our egos and
keep face—while the world convolutes and men and women die
under cobblestones, their lament worn on our shiny coats

Conscious of my co-workers, who, like me, were summoned here
to learn about realism
in a world that works with codes, saying one thing but really
meaning another
I scribble unconscious thoughts on my note pad

"She said that in an empathic voice looking at me. I thought she really meant it.

I shared my experience and voiced my real opinion about the matter of handling emergency calls with passion and anger in my voice. I apologized for being so overtly crude calling out in my native way. She said there was no need to apologize, she appreciates my outspokenness. She said that our hospital is one that values diversity of opinion and manners."

It has happened before—many times—for I cannot contain the words that want to speak, if I try to do that, I feel I am going to explode and my heart throbs like a lion as if telling me that I must stand up and speak, speak the words that mean, speak the words that shine and walk and do things

When the first speaker starts presenting his version of truth, and I really feel he has good intentions, I stare at the word "Courage," the first on his list and I imagine what it really means, writing things in my head, so that I do not forget

Moving down his impressive list, he unveils another word, another value to espouse in this great organization of ours: "Dignity"

And then another: "Illumination"

And another: "Respect"

I take all his words and I compose a phrase, which then becomes a full poem, and then, because the axiom is still to be fully revealed and pushes the pen to extend itself, I am forced to write an entire novel where the truth can really be explored and the mask unmasked

The whole day goes by and I have spent it writing a treaty on
truth missing the message of the speaker, who is an expert on the
matter—and they have paid for me to be here

At the end I am asked to share my opinions about the value of the
workshop
With my heart throbbing, the lion running after the prey, I get up
and speak
reading from the full novel that I wrote

They look at me and try to interrupt my current of thought
The axiom that I want to announce which evades neat phrases
full of splendid adjectives
I babble and babble in the tongue that really speaks, wants to
speak
The lion inside me is appeased, exhausted by the adventure

The next day I am summoned by the Chief
She is an efficient woman who has made it all the way to the very
top
She is also an expert on diversity (she comes from a society where
hierarchies are sharp and has written a book on how Canada
must learn from other societies)
I sit in her office and she gives me a notice of layoff in a calm
controlled rhetoric

Because the lion inside me is throbbing again I say, "Call me
paranoid but I can't help thinking that there is a link between my
layoff and my outspokenness. You know, my parents grew up in
a fascist country. They knew that if they spoke, they would go to
jail or even be killed. They knew the lion because the lion did not
hide itself and so they found protection however they could in
order not to choke inside the lie and be eaten by the beast. Here

the matter appears in another way. The lion tells you to speak
and exercise your democratic rights but that is only bait to fool
the innocent, for when you really speak, the lion bites you and
throws you out of its reign. This lion, Madam, is a tricky one."

I go on and on, unimpeded by the code, until she calls security to
escort me out
I am officially unemployed not because I am lazy
and not because there is no work for me given that I am
multiskilled
and highly interdisciplinary—two skills currently valued given
the fragility of
our economy that demands mobility and adaptability, the
Minister of Labour recently announced, reminding us that he
himself was once a taxi driver

I am officially unemployed not because I am lazy
And not because there is no work for me
But because I speak

I speak

Forgive me for this obsession
For I cannot help it
I was born with words staring at me and calling me out
Begging me to act on their behalf so that they don't lose voice
And the idea can still be spotted somewhere

Words calling me out
I see "vagabond" on the high placard anchored on the Bay Street
tower
And I call the story behind it, writing on any empty surface that I
can find around me
Scribbles where the truth is pushing to come out

I was born a mystic
Enchanted by syllables that then call words
And poems, and essays, and treaties and novels
Like a never-ending train travelling to the beautiful land
Where speaking, between you and I, truly takes place
Without rhetorical currents vaulting its bursting force

I see "sky"—and I search for a pen
To write the yet untold

It is not my fault
It is the lion calling me
Commanding my throbbing heart

The Stairs

I sit under the stairs of an old church
Silence raining down on me

I watch the dance of people awakening to the clarity of summer
and the hydrangeas in their gardens—flowers brought from
another continent to remind oneself of the old house where we
began to understand the world

I sit under the stairs of an old church
Smiling at the world and at God—who made it all happen

Magnificent circle surrounding us

Me and you

Never alone in this garden of light and footsteps
And the silver smiles of enchanted children born yesterday
Beautiful marvellous pearls engendered by the pulse of the
universe
And the willingness of love

Under starry wintry nights
When the breeze is proper
And the hug eternal

Mark Me and Paint Me and Make Me

Mark me and paint me, see me in the insides of my insides where I dance swallows and sparrows crying the sorrows of my dead father and my soon to disappear mother in winged sky movements that overtake all my limbs, my bones disappearing into the voluptuous circle of life

Mark me and paint me, see me inside the inside of my protruding hill where rivers swallow pure water and you sing excruciating love to the minor realms of my back bones, I twisting in shadows and curving in wells of myrtle smells and bewitching carnations, vivid reds and greens pulverizing my every surface with liquid pure wisdom

I am painted because you paint me—I am a rainbow, a window that comes out only at night under the luminous wings of the stars and the prayers of the night gods, those stunning inflamed flamingos that fly from the cost of Mozambique to bring uncanny light to my starving soul

I am painted because you spent an entire night staring upon me, in deep awe, in deep love, spraying silvery colours and bronze moons under my skin, way beyond the first circle of the well to enter the other mornings, the infinite seasons, meeting meaning, meeting soul on the backs of running translucent transfigured birds

I am painted, I am marked with petals of night rainbows and shadows from the Indian sea of austral Africa, I become Maputo, the city, the pearl of light, inundated with sparkling marvels and happy sorrows, the *saudade* for the eternal, singing the beautiful revolution with bleeding gorgeous red carnations found in

your garden and mine in that night of deliverance, pure souls
serenading to the sinners, all screaming absolution like pure
impassioned priests gesticulating in mad beauty, the belief found
at the bottom of the enlightened pit of consciousness after years
of blindness

I am painted because you paint me, calling all my beautiful
shades to the surface, stunning the onlookers and making vast
the eyes of children

Without you—there is nothing and I cry poor under my bare
clothes, the black colours of a lonely window

My Source

My source is wide like the plains, vast like the sky, open, open like large As and Os, without consonants interrupting the free flow, except perhaps the Y because it too is grand and expansive like the full moon in a night in cold high January when I freeze under the sky, eyes open, head tilted to astonishment

It begins way back, beyond the river, behind the sun, under the tree of the great oak

I call it to myself with the frequency of a doubting dark existentialist, a dumb pessimist who cannot just be, always whining, always showing off trying to be intelligent throwing around the bad spells of the nihilists as it they were golden axiomatic truths, only because I too have too much bread to eat and no children to feed, only because I too have allowed boredom to execute my days

But I am not sick, I am not alone, I am not doomed, I am not broken

There is Bach and Vivaldi, there is the morning dawn and the night candour
And the imperceptible freckle on the left side of your right cheek
And the cats and the rabbits and the night owls and my little dog Pintas whose green eyes are like live emeralds found at the bottom of my own self when I look into him and we both know who we are, opaqueness breaks and water is all there is

Immersed in the silence that pounds in my chest, I gather force to call the roots, pulling water, drinking leaves, pushing the sun to my trunk so that moss and moisture can grow and then the rest will surely come because the base is where everything starts

I call myself invoking words that I know, sacred ritualistic mumblings that have been used by many people and also words that are new—just born in that very moment, still warm and smelling of mother's milk, words that speak, that growl and cry, calling the beautiful, summoning the absent with a magic that brings everything to life, blind no more

I descend down there through a language that I summon, that I know deeply, sinking into thought, into body, into soul—calling seas, calling birds, calling the first matter and the great wild dogs that bite with the viscerality of the hungry for life and bread and days to come, endless lines of mornings that give sun to the limbs allowing them to dance and crawl till the end of time, children engaged in the possessing game of life

I descend down there through a language that I summon—I see veins and roots and rivers, I see suns and moons, sweet grapes for my tongue, I see the sharp edges of comets speeding to disappear into black matter

I see my mother screaming, her legs wide, suffering in agony to bring me to this world because her love is grand

I know the source—for now—because She is still alive

One day, when she goes, I may become lost, meandering through the agony of lack, sky with no suns, no moons, no wolves, no comets, the absence of a hand to kiss, of an arm to hold

I mourn you already mama when I should only celebrate you
I mourn you already mama when I should only call you to speak the word
The beautiful language that we both know—embedded in the threshold of our every cell

The Rescue of Birds

When the day breaks, I feel the light in each surface of my body
Spring food telling me that the birds are indeed alive in the
recesses of my most dark parts, those centimeters of my being
that occasionally forget the dance of the stars and the lilies of the
large endless valleys

When the day breaks, I am summoned to encounter in me the
pollen that still remains from last spring when the birds came
down again to find flowers and forge nests

I am summoned by the gods of life, who despite all, refuse to give
in and continue to say "Yay" and refuse "Nay"

I am summoned by life
In this day of grave revelations and sad news from Libya

My Life

My life has come to me from faraway lands
From Russian Gulags and Egyptian deserts
The oppressive heat and the gelid cold intertwined in one single
sheet
To give me the flavours of life and memories of different people

My life has come to me via rapid and slow trains travelling to and
from the neverlands
Moving engines full of passengers with languid eyes staring at
the windows of their own lives and those of others—like stunned
domesticated cats who have forgotten how to hunt

My life has come to me through the inflated veins of my mother
And the waters of my dead father, a river of red and colourless
magnum that only runs straight and never looks back

I have dreams of my life intertwined with dreams of yours
I have them often, as if my beautiful mind, or what some call the
soul, has never been alone and always possessed, in the memory
that it holds, fragments of all lives that have walked on earth

As if a film that knows no end and no beginning

Or a gigantic aorta whose blood never dries up, jumping from
one body to the other
And transporting with it the remembrance of an entire species
and even the thoughts of animals

For have you not seen the colour of the frog or the red of the chicken when you kill them for your own survival, have you not eaten their flesh and their blood making it yours and have you not entered their dreams through the bone when masticating their sacred flesh?

—You have

And even if you are a vegetarian, it's all the same, for flowers and oak trees also have blood, even though transparent like limpid water, like the soul of God speaking to you via a see-through mirror

My life is yours, for everything is a lace of unending songs and cries
Only to make sure that no one is ever really alone, and most importantly,
To let you know the sorrow that the world carries in its belly
So that you do not forget how to be kind

And feed the birds,

Those flying stunning creatures
Who roam outside, running away from their homeland
Where hunger plagues the fields
And sectarian groups attack the mercy of life

Refusing Fame

I live hidden in somber caves, dressed in dark unnoticeable clothes so not to disturb peace and the right to be

I wander through single coloured gardens with unadorned murals, unlike King Sun who continuously suffered from grandiose dreams and made his subjects crawl down under the massive stones they were erecting to fulfill madness and pure injustice, before the revolution came and screamed from the bottom of the human soul

I cover my beautiful body with sturdy sheets to hide the stunning excellence I am made of because I do not want dogs barking at me and undressing me with their teeth

I do all this and my liberated friends say that I suffer from profound Catholic repression, the type that only Salazar and his bishop friends were capable of engendering

I smile when they say that, a quiet hidden smile that only my inner soul is capable of reading—I smile and I think: "If only they could see, if only my god were to speak to them, then perhaps the world would be less brilliant and so much more fundamental."

I roam the streets when it's the most quiet so not to disturb the breathing that ascends from me when all is in order and the nether is reachable with my finger tips

I make myself ugly and crouch down my height so that the paparazzi will leave me alone and I can live in solace through the fields of my being, like a happy butterfly that knows all too well

that life on the fast lane of the world runway is not to be envied—
only to be avoided—yes, because she remembers how it was when
she was just a worm condemned to the baseness of life

I summersault the big scenes when I sense their thundering noise
breaking my hymen

I lay down for the prince to pass so that I can tell him that blued
blood is no longer in fashion and I laugh at the magazines and the
bees behind them sculpting perfection at the imperfect perfect
and intruding with the true light of the world

I go to different stores every day and walk through different
streets so that no one recognizes me and I can fully feel who I am

I refuse fame to become truly famous: I am not an imposter

I refuse fame because I want to rely on the membrane of my
inner bone marrow to remember who I am and how I am

I am the daughter of the people
The saint of bread and water

My mother is a peasant woman selling goat cheese
To the important judges of Selanjal

I am—fully, without your glitter and silver turning me into
a transvestite of nothingness

The Long Boots of the Cowboy

He walks around spiting the tip of his feet
Like a snake ready to attack the unaware princess who might be
walking through the desert looking for doves or white roses—
those secrets of the eternal that we often encounter in the barest
of places

He crosses the sliding hills of the Western Americanized deserts
fully sure that the land upon which he walks is his private farm,
so even the insects, which might call that terrain their home, are
left smashed by the force of his iron boots

He walks in dancing, capable and able movements, spreading
himself widely through that land so full of visible life, the
sentients of this world—those who walk slowly and humbly for
they know that the universe is abundant in life, in breaths, and
sighs, in colours, and enlightened shades

He walks unaware
Oblivious to the yearnings of the princess, the stories of the
Indians, the beautiful wildness of staring moving horses on their
way to the river, to the channel, to the lake

Acknowledgments

I would like to thank all the poets and language makers that I have read and continue to read, who inspire me and move me to see beyond my limited capacities—those magicians who strive to create a clean, potent and able language that can enhance our vision and call out a rhetoric that disallows humanity, love and collectivity. My gratitude to you, Clarice Lispector, and you Luce Irigaray, for that special love that you allow to be envisioned when you put your words together and form a new script, which is a new vision, a new way of living and loving—a philosophy that our world desperately needs.

My gratitude also goes to M G Vassanji, Nurjehan Aziz and all Mawenzi House staff for editing, publishing and promoting my work. To be willing to publish poetry in our moment is no small feat.

Thank you to the Insomniac Press and the Ontario Arts Council for the Writers' Reserve grant for the completion of this work.